# The Collective Truth

## Volume I

Mano Sotelo

*The Collective Truth*™

All biblical quotations are taken from the New
American Bible.

Published by Wheatmark™
2030 East Speedway Blvd., Suite 106
Tucson, Arizona 85719 U.S.A.
www.wheatmark.com

Publisher's Cataloging-In-Publication Data
(Prepared by The Donohue Group, Inc.)

Collective Truth.
  The collective truth. Volume 1 / [The Collective
Truth].

    p. : ill. ;  cm.

  Work attributed to an entity calling itself The
Collective Truth.
    ISBN-13: 978-1-58736-757-1
    ISBN-10: 1-58736-757-2

1. Spiritual life.  2. Ego (Psychology)—Religious as-
pects.  3. Self-actualization (Psychology)

B841.C65 2007
204.2    2006938721

rev202501

# *Contents*

# *No New Concepts*

This world offers many religions, philosophers, theorists, mystics, political organizations, self-help books, sacred texts, scientific formulas, and analyses; yet so many people who utilize these tools continue to struggle. They struggle for peace, enlightenment, or salvation. Why is that?

The objective of this book is to promote an awareness of what is real. Through this awareness the truth is revealed. Heaven is now. In fact, lasting peace and paradise have been accessible all along.

So where do we start? First by saying that there is no mystery to be solved. The road to awareness is accessible to everyone.

You don't need to go to any particular place

to practice or pray. You don't need to join this or that organization. You won't find enlightenment in anyone or in any book, including this one. Ultimately, the only place where you will find salvation is within yourself.

This book is merely a map. A book of diagrams to remind you of the illusion we participate in. None of these concepts is new. None of them is revolutionary. Loving, peaceful concepts have been around for many, many years.

There is nothing mystical about these words and images. This is not a sacred text or a book of set ideologies. This type of thinking or practice has been repeated throughout history. Yet it has never provided lasting results for anyone. Instead, this is simply a book of awareness. A collection of thoughts derived from thoughtful daily living. Thoughts ultimately leading us toward the truth.

# *The Ego and Waking from the Dream*

What is the dream? To answer that, we must first look to the ego.

1. The ego is who we think we are. The ego latches onto roles, appearances, and possessions, and then makes value judgments.

What are roles? Roles are positions you hold at work, in organizations, in school, or at home, and they often demand a certain set of behaviors. But if I ask you to describe yourself, do the words *student, doctor, librarian, cashier, mother,* or *father* really encapsulate who you are?

The ego also makes value judgments about

roles. It says, *I value a doctor more than a nurse, a store owner more than a sales clerk.*

Ask people "Who are you?" and they sometimes think that by adding more titles they can increase the legitimacy and value of their answer. So they might answer, "I'm a forty-five-year-old Hispanic accountant. I'm a Christian, a father, and a baseball coach." Or "I'm an Irish female punk rock musician and a student at Harvard Law School." These answers are limiting and inaccurate. True, these are roles and descriptions, but they don't truly answer the question "Who are you?"

The truth is that you are a precious living being, basically no different from any other. You breathe air, eat food, and drink water. You want to feel happy, and you would prefer to avoid suffering.

Most especially, you *are*. Therefore you are part of God. Everything is a part of God; however, you specifically have the capacity to experience the consciousness that links everything.

2. The ego establishes what we value in

ourselves and in others. Things of value might include appearance and material possessions.

Does having a lot of money in your bank account make you a better person than when you had only a few dollars in the bank? Of course not; but many still value the rich over the poor.

Additionally, it is not unheard of for many people to establish their sense of worth by the type of car they drive. And although the ego may never prompt you to say it, the ego may make you think, *I have a luxury automobile and you ride the bus; therefore, you are less than me.*

Appearance reinforces the ego by focusing on such things as gender, race, age, clothing, or a sense of style. So the ego may say, *You are fat, and I am skinny; therefore, I am better than you.*

Many times the ego just wants more. For the ego there is never enough. Therefore, the ego also latches onto abstract concepts such as achievement, gain, best, and success. As a result, people controlled by their egos spend most of their time in the future or past, rarely in the present moment.

3.  The ego is that part of our psyche that separates us from one another. It is the false sense of "I" that says, *You are separate from me. I am Christian, you are Muslim, and we are both separate from God.*

So when looking at these examples of how the ego functions, we can ask the question "Why does the ego do this?" It does this for survival, control, greed, fear, and a false sense of need. The ego creates a countless number of stories. Let us look at one quick example.

A child is born today, and the parents immediately see the child's upbringing as a means to an end.

The child is raised to *succeed* academically in order to be able to go to the *best* college. This is done so that they might *achieve* greatness within the most *desirable* occupation, ultimately to be *deemed* the "most *valuable* person" possible.

The same child, as an adult, will continue to try to increase his sense of worth. He will do this by *striving* to accumulate money, possessions, notoriety, and friends. All the while, he may worship and amass as many prayers as possible to *become* a "*better* person" and *attain* enlightenment.

So what is the dream?

The dream is the illusion created and sustained by the ego. The illusion that we are not perfect right now. It is our false sense of reality. It is everything most people embrace as the truth.

So how do you get beyond this dream? Think critically about your thoughts. That is, reflect upon what you have been told is, or what you perceive to be, the truth.

Most of our everyday thoughts (i.e., associations, opinions, etc.) are ego driven. So when you reflect upon your thoughts, you will eventually find the ego. In observing the ego, you will begin to see how most of our realities are spent within the mind. This is the dream.

Being conscious of this illusion will enable you to make the constant choice whether or not to awake from the dream.

# DIAGRAMS FOR
# SECTION I

DIAGRAM I

# Which one is better?

DIAGRAM 1

Which one is better?

Of the children around the world who are born every second, do we ever ask this question?

Yes, if the ego is involved, historically we have. We somehow manage to measure each baby's value.

Maybe a movie star's baby is more important than a baby born to an average person. Or maybe a baby born to a traditional family is more important than one born to a single parent. If we say these statements are absurd, then why do we watch and buy material that supports this thinking?

There are many places around the world that still value a male child over a female. Why? Because a male in that society can probably make more money, thus feeding the ego's hunger for more. Second, the male will pass on the family name, feeding the ego's need for survival through producing a sense of immortality.

DIAGRAM I

To the question above, we may reply, "No, we never ask which one is better." Indeed, many people view all children as precious. So why is it that when these children reach the ages of five, ten, twenty, thirty we can easily make value judgments about them? We say, "He's a child prodigy," "She's a rebellious teenager," "He's a lazy good-for-nothing," and so on.

Does the ability to assess someone's value become easier with age? The ego would respond *yes*. Why is that?

The ego finds less utility to measure in a child. Second, the ego in the child has not yet fully developed. So there is less for our ego to react to. When the ego in the child finally does develop, other egos will either react to it or feed off of it.

It is important to remember that we are all precious. All life is precious, and that is a constant.

*We are all products of conditioning.*
*Our perceptions and values*
*reflect our egos.*

*A willingness to see beyond this*
*will point you to the truth.*

Diagram 2

| | |
|---|---|
| Man | Woman |
| Father | Mother |
| Money Maker | Wife |
| Leader | Lawyer |
| Boss | Housewife |
| Wise | Beautiful |
| Stupid | Ugly |
| Doctor | Fat |
| Brother | Thin |
| Soldier | Fashionable |
| American | Consumer |
| Korean | Talented |
| Catholic | Lesbian |
| Atheist | Social Security Number |
| Republican | Japanese |
| Successful | Child Bearer |
| Friend | Care Giver |
| Foe | Sex Object |

# Mental Labels

DIAGRAM 2

We label ourselves and others every day. Why? Because it makes us feel better about ourselves. Our labels give us a sense of purpose. We use them to compare ourselves with others and for declaring our own sense of usefulness in society.

The collective ego says that a person must have a purpose to be seen as valuable. But is this true? Does a person really need a purpose to have value? Look at one-year-old children. What purpose should they have?

Labels and roles give us a false sense of being connected to one another. Roles make us feel useful to others. As your sense of utility increases, so does your sense of self-worth. On the other hand, as we label others with a sense of utility, our own sense of value is lowered or raised.

Mental labels become physical labels, and these become our way of gauging one's importance. We are not free in this state. We bind ourselves and each other when we tie each other to labels. This becomes our identity, our belief system, and our reality.

DIAGRAM 2

If we believe our labels and live them out, then that is all we will ever be.

The thought of yourself, who you think you are, keeps you bound. When believing in this illusion, you are kept from seeing who you really are.

Your sense of self, the ego, can be difficult to overcome, as it has a personality and a lifestyle. The ego is in love with this mental image. If you see through the ego and do not believe in it, it will die. Of course, the ego does not want to die, so your sense of self keeps you prisoner.

*You must truly forgive others
and yourself
if you are to live in the present moment.*

*To hold onto associations and opinions
is to live in the past or future.*

DIAGRAM 3

Value

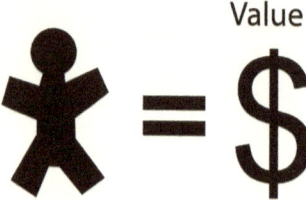

**This person possesses:**
Talent
Skills
Network of friends
Fame - Popular
Money
Same beliefs
Job title

No Value

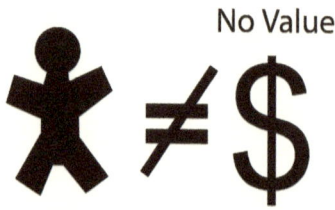

**This person possesses none
of the above.**

# How do we assess someone's value?

Diagram 3

Why do we gravitate to one person versus another? Or, how do we assess someone's value? Quite simply, through their utility. How useful are they to our ego? Can we utilize or sell their talents? If they are famous or hold a job title that we deem important, can we somehow increase our value through association as their friend? Do they reinforce our own belief system? Or can we just use them for their money?

Two men, despite their sameness, are seen very differently. One, a homeless man on the street, has little value in society. In fact, he is often labeled a problem. The second, a rich and famous pop star who makes lots of money, is seen as an icon. Why? We believe in the illusion. Does the man on the bench have less value as a person? Are the words he speaks any less profound? Or is the image, the created illusion, what we are judging and reacting to?

Cease to value anything, and you will begin the see the value in everything.

Diagram 4

## Utility
### (Comparing Value)

Diagram 4

Take a moment and observe how the ego might react to the two male images. Now, which image does society view as having more value? The ego disregards the fact that these two beings are, in essence, the same. The ego sees only roles, appearances, and possessions.

Who probably makes more money? Who has more valuable possessions? Who is probably more educated? Finally, who is more likely to have power and influence?

In an instant, two significant human beings are evaluated and their utility is measured. One is valued over the other.

DIAGRAM 5

# Utility
## (Comparing Value)

Diagram 5

Take a moment and observe how the ego might react to the two female images. Is it not common for a young woman to be preferred over an elderly woman?

Possibly we give the older woman respect because of her years of experience and presumed wisdom. Or we might give a person with a disability respect due to the challenges they might endure.

But all of these labels are quickly disregarded when the ego evaluates the utility of the person. Who is more beautiful, more able-bodied, more educated to the technology of today? The old and disabled woman cannot work or move or be like the younger woman—or can she? Have we asked them, or are these the limitations we have created for them?

Cease to label and evaluate people, and their significance will become clear.

Diagram 6

# Mental Positions

DIAGRAM 6

*I am of this nation, and you are of that one. I have my traditions, and you have yours. I believe this, and you believe that. My ways are better than yours. If they were not, why would I hold onto them so tightly?*

Societies cling to their cultures and traditions because this gives their members a sense that they belong. It offers a sense of safety, control, and prosperity. It protects them from the world. It traps them with language and customs. It offers commodities to sell to the world.

As long as we see ourselves as separate nations, that is exactly what we will be—separate. The ego will not allow us to join as one, because it needs a sense of identity in order to survive. As long as we feed into the belief of "mine and yours," we will never see clearly that you and I are the same.

If we put aside our mental positions and see ourselves solely as living beings, we will not stop living. We, in fact, will be free. We will move from our fixed positions and clearly see the one world that unites us all.

DIAGRAM 7

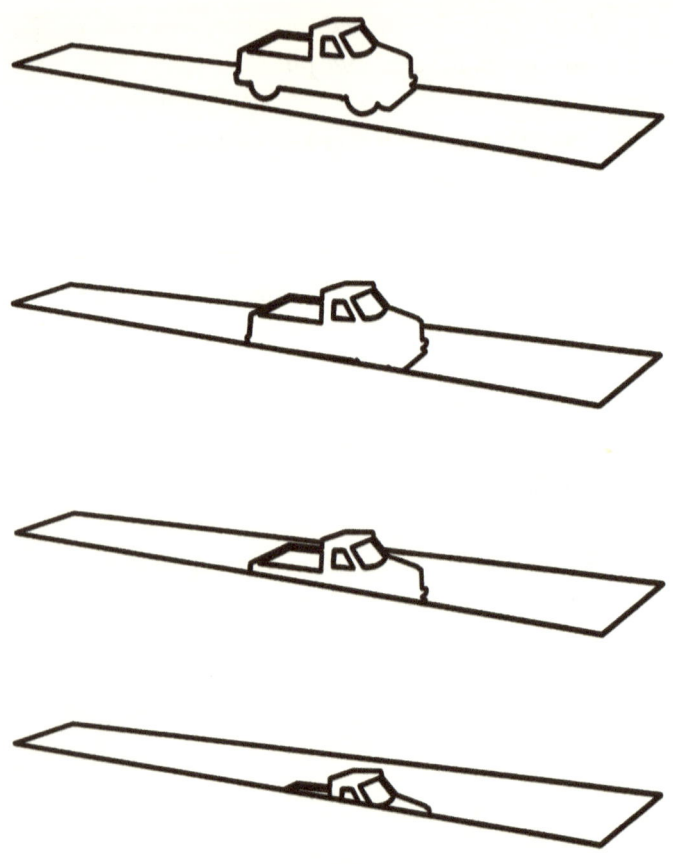

# The effects of repeated action.

DIAGRAM 7

Repeated action is like playing with a toy truck in the dirt. Every time you repeat an action, it is like you are moving the truck over the same path. Each time the truck is pushed over the path, the path grows deeper. Soon the path will turn into a rut, with walls that grow higher with each pass.

Eventually, the path becomes too deep. You have no choice but to travel the same path and take the same action. You are a captive of your own conditioning.

When we walk into a repeat situation, it is history repeating itself. If you know you are about to replay the same action, why move forward? Are you conscious or unconscious?

Maybe you are given the same situation to try something new? What if you observed the groove from above before driving into it? Is this possible?

You are not trapped, and you can avoid suffering. Stop and, before you react, still your mind. Looking at your actions from a

DIAGRAM 7

distance will give you a whole new perspective. If you are conscious, you can choose.

The groove is an illusion, constructed by your choice of behavior.

*Let go of all perceived obstacles.*
*The ego needs conflict to survive.*

DIAGRAM 8

# **Practice or Play?**

DIAGRAM 8

What have we done to our childhood games?

We no longer play. Instead we occupy ourselves with scholarships, tournaments, professional leagues, world champions, and sports icons. To what ends? To feed the ego with more money, power, and fame.

Titles and possessions are transient. Achieving, gaining, and becoming are like chasing the wind. No thing can make you more than you already are.

Observe life outside of the ego, where there is...

> no need for achievement;
> no need for ambition;
> no need for winners or losers;
> no need for reward.

Be like a child and just play. Enjoy life.

DIAGRAM 9

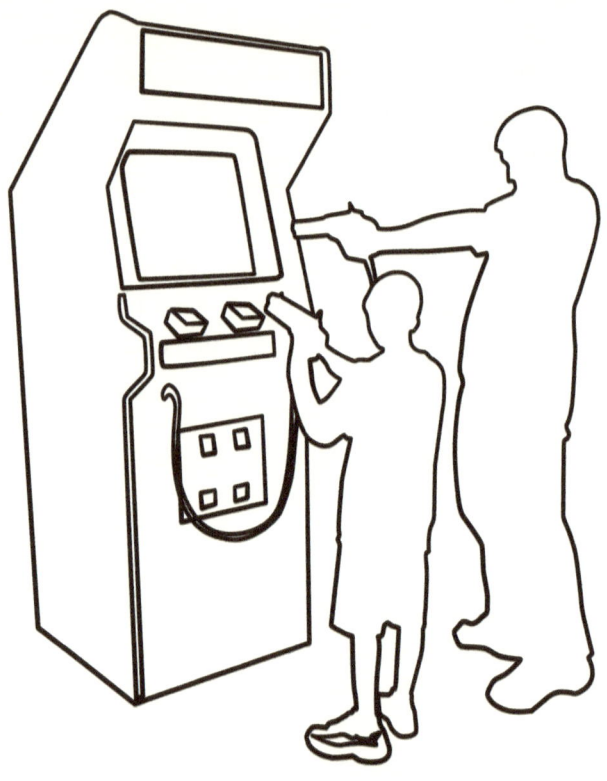

Teach by example.

DIAGRAM 9

Many people play video games with their children. Many of these games are violent. It is not uncommon for the player to be rewarded for killing others in the game. Yet it is acceptable to call this entertainment.

Think about what you are doing.

Your child is learning that this type of action is acceptable. They become desensitized to the very idea of what they are actually acting out.

In the developing ego, these images shape our children's realities. Concepts such as "respect for life" and "entertainment" become blurred.

What is this teaching your child? Is this contributing to a conscious or unconscious reality?

Our children are our mirrors. Whether we know it or not, we initially create the foundations for what they deem as real.

Teach by example. Every moment of every day, your actions are a model more powerful than any set of words or rules.

Diagram 10

# Perception and Utility.

DIAGRAM 10

The being of this person is the same, be she six or twenty years of age. Yet society labels and assigns her a different level of utility in each image. What about her does the ego use to gauge utility? Her roles and, in this example, mostly her appearance. Society has dictated to her what she should be. If she were to become fat, she would fall into yet another box or role, and so on.

The essence of this person has become lost. We begin to see nothing more than an object. One day she will be sixty-five, and her usefulness yet again will have changed.

Do we have the right to label people throughout their lives? Aren't we more than what others want us to be?

In the position of the observer or the observed, we have the potential to free one another.

Diagram 11

# Escaping Conditioning

DIAGRAM 11

As children, we are told to treat each other as equals. To value love above sex. To value the inner qualities of a person. To not judge a person by his or her appearance.

Yet, as adults, we continue to create and watch television commercials, movies, video games, and print advertisements that sell sex. In addition to this, pornography continues to be a multibillion dollar industry.

What are we, society, teaching our children to value?

In the midst of all this, observe that the ego must constantly *have*. It must constantly be doing. It will always want more.

On the level of ego, we are completely blind. We cannot see that we are hurting and limiting not only ourselves but everyone and everything around us. We trap people into roles from which they have no escape. They are as steeped in the illusion as we are.

When we believe in the dream together, we are blind together. Stop being blind.

DIAGRAM 11

Look beyond the image your ego creates. Look at your thoughts and question your conditioning. By questioning your thoughts, you become less seduced by them.

You are asleep when the ego is controlling your thoughts. It is time to wake up.

*As long as you see labels,*
*you will continue to separate*
*yourself from everything else.*

DIAGRAM 12

**Staying centered and at peace.**

In a world of diversions.

Diagram 12

How did we get to the point of having to be constantly entertained? Do we really need constant stimuli? Can we function without our distractions?

This world is full of diversions. Some are acquired from our upbringing, and social environment. Some are sought out to hide pain and anger.

This human world is for the ego an all-you-can-eat buffet, and we are the creators of every dish being served. We love our illusions, and the deeper we are in the dream, the more difficult it can be to wake up.

We hold the belief that we are "things." We are appearances, roles, and a collection of possessions. Therefore, we believe that we need things. We are trained to think this way; yet we are born with nothing and will die with nothing.

So how do you stay centered?

First, observe all these diversions. They all keep you within yourself. That is, they keep

DIAGRAM 12

you trapped within the thinking mind. If you are in your mind, you are in the dream. The dream of evaluating objects, moments, and needs.

"To evaluate" implies that there must be a *good* and a *bad*. In this polarity, there can never be lasting peace.

Second, be present. The ego cannot survive if you are fully attuned to the present moment. So the ego will keep you occupied within the future or past; and when these states of mind are no longer stimulating, it will fill your present time with diversions. The ego will say, *Give me anything to stimulate my mind, as long as I don't have to be still.*

Still your mind, and you find the center, which is the present moment. It is here you will find no wanting, or more specifically, lasting peace.

*Accept life continuously*
*and you will never find conflict.*

DIAGRAM 13

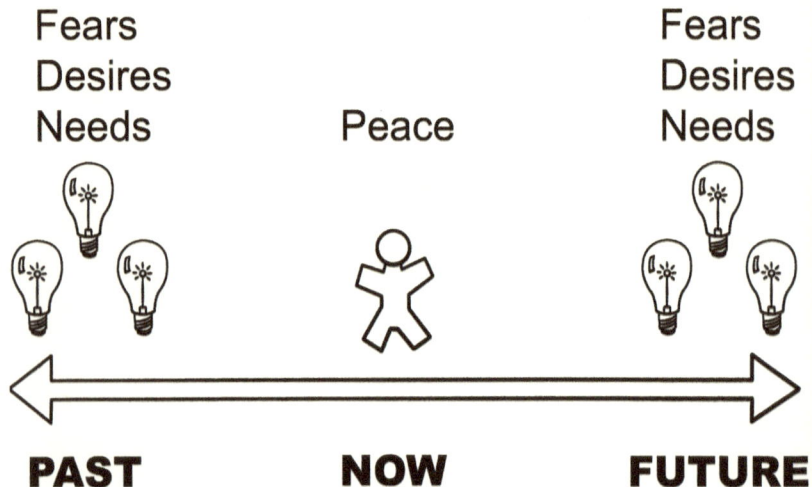

Diagram 13

Think of your fears, desires, and needs. Are they now, in the present moment? Most fears, desires, and needs derive out of our thoughts and perceptions of past and future events.

We want this or that to ensure that we are happier in the future. We need or fear things in response to what we were taught or experienced in the past.

But do either of these realities reflect the truth of the present moment?

When you desire a vacation or a product on television, are you focusing on the present moment? Or are you using the present moment as a means to reach what you desire?

When you meet someone and you begin to experience stress, are you responding to them at the present moment? Or are you subconsciously thinking of a past encounter with someone similar to them?

Maybe you are placing a label on them that corresponds to something you fear or dislike.

DIAGRAM 13

For example, you might use labels of authority, gender, race, or religious background.

On the other hand, if you find that your fear, desire, and need do not derive out of the past or future, it is sure to project you into one or the other. For example, if you say, "I am hungry," this need will project your thoughts away from the present moment in an effort to find a solution.

Ultimately, fear, desire, and need are illusions the ego generates in your mind to keep you trapped in the dream. The ego generates these emotions by pulling your mind into the past and pushing your thoughts into the future. We believe these emotions to be our reality. But the truth is that there is only the present moment.

In the present moment, when your thinking mind is still, all is perfect.

*All problems arise
from a wandering mind.*

DIAGRAM 14

## MAN VIEWING THE STREAM OF LIFE.

● = The things and people in your life.

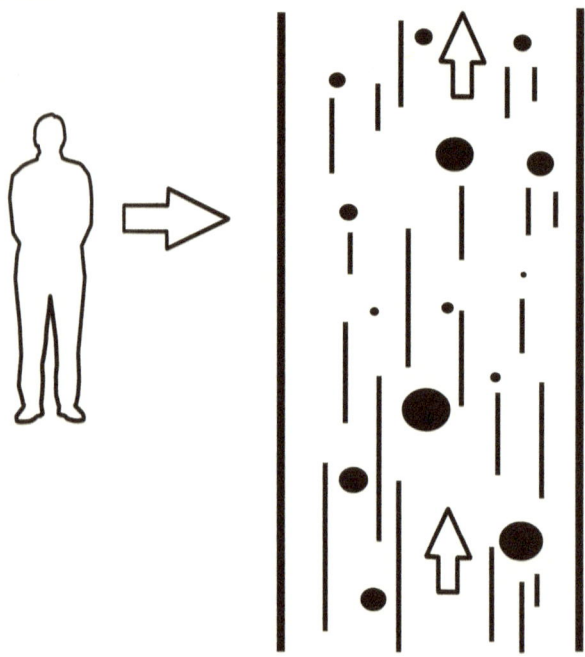

# Refrain from fixing your thoughts.
# All things are transient.

Diagram 14

If you live in the ego, then your thoughts will often be fixed. That is, you will often perceive things to be a certain way as opposed to observing them as they truly are. In this dream, people and things must stay the same in order for you to retain a sense of happiness.

This is the trap that many couples fall into. Each partner's thoughts are fixed, but they fail to realize that the world, including their partner and themselves, is changing. Once your partner falls outside of your fixed ideas of what an ideal partner should be, then the relationship begins to fall apart.

Do not fix your thoughts. Moreover, stop the initial mental concept of the thing you are observing. Simply still your mind, and you will see that the stream of life, although ever changing, is always perfect.

DIAGRAM 15

# Family:
## a loving or unloving image?

DIAGRAM 15

We have conditioned our minds to think of the family unit as a collection of roles. Each member has their duty, and each has an expected behavior to follow.

The parental roles include provider, caregiver, child bearer, moneymaker, lawmaker, disciplinarian, housekeeper, and so on.

On the other hand, the child's roles may include heir, plaything, gender replica, or the representation of potential prosperity and hope.

Initially, the child will reflect any parental perception. Because this image directly reflects the egos of the parents, it binds the family together. The family image is a happy one.

But eventually, the parents' layers of pain, love, stress, suffering, status, lack, disease, hostility, anger, tears, sorrow, happiness, yelling, and hugging become implanted in their child. Now the child is the mirror of the parents.

DIAGRAM 15

This is how we reach dysfunction as units. Is this living? No wonder we break down, rebel, have family crises. No wonder teens see this unit and want to escape it. No wonder we sometimes see the family as an unhappy image.

How can we make this stop? How can we make this a loving image, one we want to give everything to and ask nothing from in return?

You must get out of your roles and place no one in a box. Look at your loved ones and see that they are so much more than a character or placeholder.

If we bind ourselves and others in roles, then we are prisoners to these roles. Freedom and imprisonment are our choices.

Be kind and loving to others and yours will always be a happy image.

*Be aware of all that you do.*

DIAGRAM 16

# Sight - Perception

DIAGRAM 16

If you focus on only what is immediately in front of you, you fail to see the bigger picture.

Take a lesson from your sight. Sight and the way we perceive things are very similar. Up close, you notice each leaf on the tree, each blade of grass, each person walking around you. They all appear as separate.

However, as your focus turns to the objects in the distance, no longer can you distinguish the leaves, the blades of grass, or the people. They have blended into one mass.

When we feel isolated all we need to do is stand back and look at the situation from a distance. By doing this, we can clearly see that all is one.

Be observant in life. All you need is before you.

DIAGRAM 17

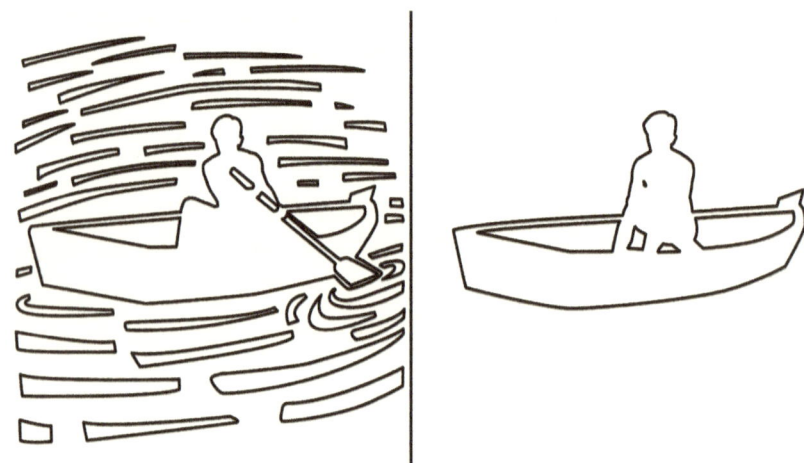

**The man that is still
and seeks no direction is at peace.**

Diagram 17

Two men sit in separate boats. One experiences resistance and physical strain. The other experiences stillness and peace. Why is this so?

The person who sits still, empties his mind, is conscious of the moment, and experiences the world with all the senses is the person who will find peace. This person will smell the fresh air, enjoy the wind on his face, and appreciate the beauty that surrounds him. He will notice how his body feels, and at once realize that the world, including himself, emanates peace.

The second person's ego has grown tired of the moment and seeks something more fulfilling. His paddle touches the water, and turbulence is manifested through splashes, ripples, and waves. He paddles in the direction he seeks and is not conscious of the turbulence he has created. Agitation now passes through the water and himself.

Here in this diagram, the ship represents the person. The water represents life. Some days are smooth and some days stormy. Who is

DIAGRAM 17

manifesting these emotions? If we seek a "better place," does our desire create peace or turbulence?

Enjoy life. Be still in everything and know all is God.

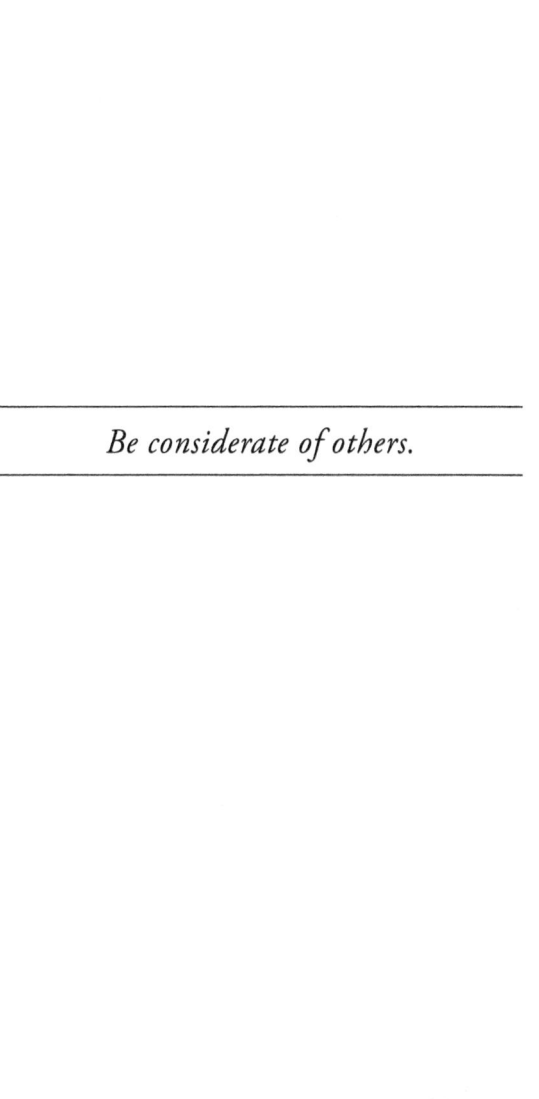

*Be considerate of others.*

DIAGRAM 18

= Mental image or concept

**For every action
there is a reaction.**

DIAGRAM 18

We react because our mind is thinking instead of observing. For instance, think about the actions that fear, desire, and need generate. From these actions, an equal reaction will follow.

Most people, when confronted with challenges, instantly react. The challenge might be verbal, physical, or mental; however, the response is usually the same instant reaction.

Think about this phenomenon. Does it foster peace or conflict?

When you react to someone else, you generate a potential reaction of opposition. This fosters conflict.

So how do we deal with difficult situations?

We simply need to wait before reacting. Just give yourself a second or two to let the moment be. That is all you need to do.

DIAGRAM 18

You will find that within this moment of stillness resolution to the conflict will become clear.

Living beyond what the ego dictates provides a world free of conflict.

*Don't be conditional.*

DIAGRAM 19

# No Right or Wrong.
## Only conscious and unconscious.

DIAGRAM 19

The light bulb in this diagram represents a mental concept. If you have a mental concept or idea of what you are experiencing, you will always distort reality.

The asleep mind, one run by the ego, is the lost mind. It is good and bad, happy and sad, rich and lacking. It is bipolar. This mind moves from extremes with little rest and little forgiveness. It reacts and is ultimately unstable.

The mind that is not led by the ego is not lost, because it has nothing to search for. The mind at rest, or not thinking about what it needs, can truly see things the way they are and be nonjudgmental. This state of mind is clear and centered.

Cease to have ideas about things. Be of no mind:

mind = thinking

thinking = emotion

emotion = good and bad moments

DIAGRAM 19

good and bad moments =
constant fluctuation

constant fluctuation = no peace

So are you conscious or unconscious? Awake
or asleep?

*We are all products of conditioning.*
*Our perceptions and values*
*reflect our egos.*

*A willingness to see beyond this*
*will point you to the truth.*

DIAGRAM 20

What is the purpose of a wave?

DIAGRAM 20

There are many similarities between humans and the rest of nature. Take humans and waves for example. Both come in many shapes and sizes. Both tend to follow a larger order. Both are temporary physical manifestations.

So when asking "what is a good person" or "what is my purpose," it might be better to ask "what is a good wave" or "what is the purpose of a wave."

What is a good wave? Should it be calm so the boat can glide over it easily? Or should it grandly break close to the shore, where the observer on the beach may truly appreciate its glory? Or should it rise to a minimum height suitable for surfing?

Do you see that all these questions only lead to how the wave will be used? The ego always equates "good" with "purpose." But the purpose changes from one user to the next. Never are all egos satisfied at once and never is the wave at peace if it is constantly trying to fill a need.

DIAGRAM 20

So what is the true purpose of a wave? There is no purpose. What is a good wave? There is no value assessment. The manifestation of the wave is enough.

*You must truly forgive others
and yourself
if you are to live in the present moment.*

*To hold onto associations and opinions
is to live in the past or future.*

DIAGRAM 21

There are no answers.
Only questions in a box.

DIAGRAM 21

You will never find all the answers you seek.

Because there are no answers.

Only questions, created by mental concepts.

Concepts created in your box.

A box you call reality.

Diagram 22

Cease to value all viewpoints.

DIAGRAM 22

Cease to seek value in viewpoints.

viewpoints = your way/my way

your way/my way = right/wrong

right/wrong = no peace

no peace = turmoil, chaos, no truth

# *Spiritual Practice*

Think of the limitations of our language or numerical system. Now, think of your thoughts about God. Can these systems quantify or measure God?

The truth can never be found in the limitations of mental concepts or viewpoints. You will always have your opinions of God, while others hold steadfast to theirs.

It is not worthwhile to debate the nature of God. Rather, if God is the truth and the truth is beyond any singular viewpoint, then God is everything.

Everything is God. Therefore, everything, whether mental or physical, is of God's spirit. When one sees this truth—that everything is spiritual—every moment becomes a spiritual practice, a practice of consciousness and of being present and in total alignment with God's manifestation.

## SCIENCE AND RELIGION

The religions and sciences of the world reflect our instinctual knowledge that there is a greater intelligence than our own. There is no debate that religion and science have helped a great many people. But at the same time, these institutions, by their organizational nature, divide the very world they strive to unite.

This book does not wish to discredit any religious or scientific organization. Nor does it embrace any singular viewpoint. Instead, this book recognizes the contributions of all religions and sciences. It is with these contributions that we find our way closer to the collective truth.

# DIAGRAMS FOR
# SECTION 2

DIAGRAM 23

Do we really believe this?

Diagram 23

What is evil? Is it the devil or a monster that lives underground? Is evil an entity to be defeated with a sword or firearm?

If you see evil as one of the above images, evil will always be an external element. Evil will always be a force to be defeated, in all the manifestations where you perceive it to be present. The problem with this is that perceptions change from person to person.

Think critically: if evil is always external to you, then there is no reason to reflect upon your negative behavior or actions.

So what then is evil? It is any harmful thought or action. When do we experience such events in our lives? When we, or someone else, are not conscious of our behavior.

Ultimately evil is the unobserved, uncontrolled ego. Be conscious of your actions, and evil will cease to be a personal obstacle.

DIAGRAM 24

## How long will you hold onto mental images of divinity?

DIAGRAM 24

The ego needs to place an appearance on divinity. One can look to mythology to see that people have done this throughout the ages.

The ego has frequently utilized the image of wings to depict the appearance of divinity. We see this in images portraying the Egyptian's phoenix. The Greek god Hermes and the Roman god Mercury are often shown wearing winged shoes and a winged cap. The Valkyries of Norse mythology are sometimes shown wearing winged helmets and riding winged horses. Finally, we can point to our current civilization's images of angels.

Is any one of these images a true or universal representation of the "divine"? Each image means something different to each person. If we are to recognize the unity among us, does an image support this vision?

Are we ready to let go of our past perceptions and be with the fact that nothing written or visual will universally quantify every thought?

DIAGRAM 24

It is time to let go of mental images of the divine so we can join together as one with that which is divine.

Look beyond mental images of the divine, and you will begin to see the divinity in all things.

*You must truly forgive others*
*and yourself*
*if you are to live in the present moment.*

*To hold onto associations and opinions*
*is to live in the past or future.*

DIAGRAM 25

Is this God?

DIAGRAM 25

Think of the movies you have seen. The television shows or commercials you have watched. The books you have read. The sports events you've seen. Do the plots, events, and actions in these experiences seem to repeat themselves?

This is not out of coincidence. The ego needs to keep you caught up in the dream, and when it thinks that you are becoming bored with its illusion, it simply reinvents itself.

Let's look at God as an example. Throughout a great portion of our modern civilization, God has been depicted as a white-skinned, white-bearded old man. First, as Odin and Zeus, God wore a winged helmet or carried a rod of lightning. Now, God continues to wear a white robe, but the helmet has been replaced with a halo.

Left alone, the ego will continue to create human images of God—images that reflect what it deems powerful and of great worth. But does a human image of God assist in understanding the truth?

DIAGRAM 25

Isn't God much more than any specific image created on one small planet in a universe of over a billion galaxies?

*Let go of all perceived obstacles.*
*The ego needs conflict to survive.*

DIAGRAM 26

Mental viewpoints

DIAGRAM 26

Look at your religion. Seeking the truth through a religion is like looking out only one window of your home. You will clearly see the wonderful outdoors, but you will only see it through your select viewpoint.

In doing so, your view will always be right and others' views will be wrong. The problem with this is that others, with a different viewpoint, will feel the same way.

All sides are witnessing the same wondrous world; but because of our mental positions, there will never be peace. The entire truth will never be revealed to any of us.

viewpoints = your way/my way

your way/my way = right/wrong

right/wrong = no peace

no peace = turmoil, chaos, no truth

# DIAGRAM 27

DIAGRAM 27

Which temple, church, or mosque provides the correct path to God?

If you selected one, who did the selecting? Was the selection made by a tradition, a past memory, or what you learned in school? Is it the one your parents told you to choose?

We may have many different ways of expressing ourselves, but we are all the same. Just as our churches, mosques, and temples are built from the same wood and stone. These materials come from the same mountain just as we come from the same God.

So how do you know which path to take? How do you ascend to the mountaintop?

If you are conscious, all roads will lead you to God. Enlightenment and peace will come to you.

If you are awake, you will understand that no matter where you are, you are already there.

DIAGRAM 28

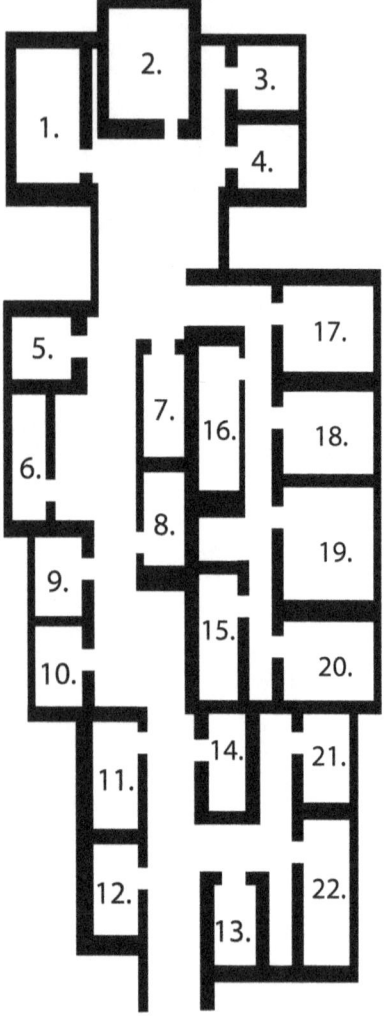

1. Christianity
2. Islam
3. Secular/
   Nonreligious/
   Agnostic/
   Atheist
4. Hinduism
5. Chinese
   traditional religion
6. Buddhism
7. Primal-indigenous
8. African
   Traditional
   & Diasporic
9. Sikhism
10. Juche
11. Spiritism
12. Judaism
13. Baha'i
14. Jainism
15. Shinto
16. Cao Dai
17. Zoroastrianism
18. Tenrikyo
19. Neo-Paganism
20. Unitarian-
    Universalism
21. Rastafarianism
22. Scientology
Etc.

DIAGRAM 28

In my Father's house there are many dwelling places. (John 14:2)

With so many different countries, political organizations, languages, cultures, traditions, and forms of artistic expression, is it any wonder that we would have more than one way of expressing our spirituality?

Everyone might have their own form of expression, but is it necessary to see each other as being separate? Or to see one as being right and the other wrong?

Are there really separate rooms in God's temple? Or is it the ego separating and comparing?

# Diagram 29

DIAGRAM 29

In regard to attaining enlightenment and peace, the ego will forever keep you looking outside of yourself. It will consistently point you in the direction of other people and places.

We build buildings and then say that this is where we will find God or that this is the best place to show our devotion to God.

But in reality we are only binding ourselves to locations, rules, and rituals. We bind ourselves and, in our illusion, forget that we are the ones holding the keys.

Still your mind. Become awake. If you wish to find a "temple" in which to find peace, look no further than yourself.

DIAGRAM 30

# The Sons and Daughters of God.

DIAGRAM 30

You must be made perfect as your heavenly Father is perfect. (Matt. 5:48)

We are all manifestations of God, divine by nature.

Yet, to our own detriment, many of us are conditioned to think that we need to search outside of ourselves to find salvation, whether this be in another person, a religious leader, or an icon.

But what is salvation?

Deliverance from evil or ruin in a future state.

If you live consciously, you will realize that the future will never come because there is always only the present moment.

If you live consciously, you will realize that your thoughts and actions are your only obstacles to peace.

DIAGRAM 30

You are the only one capable of saving your-self from suffering. So why do you wait?

Be perfect. As you are capable of being per-fect.

*As long as you see labels,
you will continue to separate
yourself from everything else.*

DIAGRAM 31

# One Reality.
Countless mental states.

DIAGRAM 31

Next time you find yourself with a group of people, ask yourself, *Presently, are we all experiencing the same emotions?*

Although you share the same space and you may be doing the same thing, it is most likely that you do not share the same emotions.

Why is that?

The ego will generate emotions—emotions created through reactions to our mental associations as opposed to the actual situation we are experiencing.

Our life, with the ego, is one lived within the mind. It is absent of any true experience. That is, we may experience new people and places; however, we are always perceiving them through the filter of our own values, beliefs, traditions, and experiences.

The mind described here can only be one of chaos and confusion. One where you are never clearly seeing what is right in front of you.

Diagram 31

Quiet your mind, and stop thinking. Experience life in the present moment, and you will find peace.

*Accept life continuously
and you will never find conflict.*

DIAGRAM 32

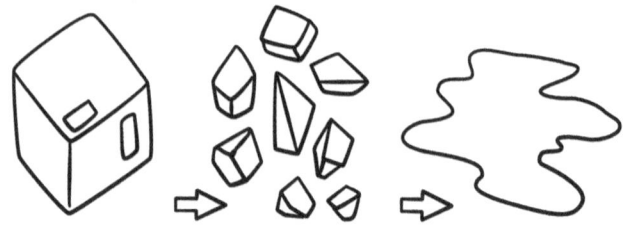

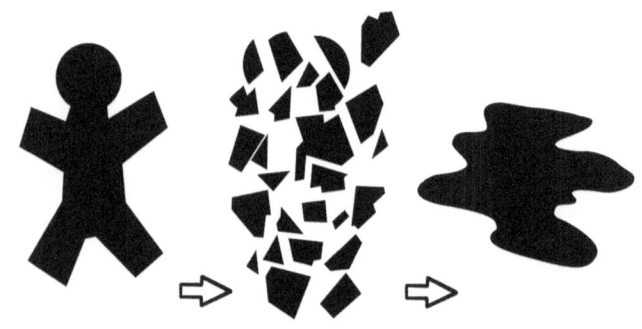

# Do not fear diversity.

DIAGRAM 32

Every day we witness new religions, political parties, organizations, educational institutions, theorists, gangs, terrorist groups, and pop culture trends come into existence.

Many see this and fear that it indicates the ever-increasing fragmentation of our society. But there is nothing to fear. The ego will fragment itself, by labels, until it cannot divide itself anymore.

Just as ice will crack into smaller pieces and eventually turn to water, so will people divide themselves back into one unit.

Imagine a rock. If you crush the rock, it will immediately break into smaller pieces. These smaller pieces represent the groups mentioned above.

At first, these smaller pieces look very different. But as you continue to crush the rock, it will become more and more fragmented until, finally, you will have turned it into a pile of dust.

Study this dust, and you will no longer see

DIAGRAM 32

the difference in the individual granules. These granules, like the separate interest groups, will no longer appear so different.

In observing the outcome of the entire process, you will see that again you have one united mass. A pile of dust from one rock— one reunification of people.

Do not fearfully react to the change that happens in the world. Nonreaction will help it come to rest.

*All problems arise
from a wandering mind.*

DIAGRAM 33

# Heaven

# Hell

Diagram 33

Make no mistake, heaven is now. But so is hell. It is our individual perceptions that make it so.

If we live in a hellish mental state, this will be reflected outwardly. Our mental chaos directly becomes our reality.

So, if we choose to continue living a life of illusion, one filled with concepts of good/bad, rich/poor, well/sick, friend/foe, our everyday living will reflect these choices. We will find ourselves, sooner or later, living in hell.

On the other hand, we can experience heaven. This is the mind at rest, with no mental conflicts—only peace.

This is most evident in nature. Notice that, with all our wars and abuse, nature maintains a constant presence. It does not fight, push, or have anger. Why? Because it has no ego. It just is. And it will outlive the human race because of this peace, for it makes no effort to preserve itself.

If there is no ego in the actions you take, only

DIAGRAM 33

peace will remain. Life is what we choose it to be: heaven or hell. It is a constant choice we make.

*Be aware of all that you do.*

DIAGRAM 34

# A world of polarity.
### (Right and wrong action,
### moving forward or backward)

**Hell**　　　　　　　　　　　　　　**Heaven**

# A world of enlightenment.
### (Awake or asleep to reality)

DIAGRAM 34

The top diagram shows our present sense of reality. It is one of polarity, one of suffering and happiness.

In this reality, we must constantly strive, or search, to become enlightened. We find ourselves fluctuating between opposite poles, and our lives are never at rest. We never find lasting peace.

In this world of polarity, heaven is a distant world. Even the idea that Earth will someday be like heaven always seems out of reach. Is this reality? For most of us it is, because we believe in the polarity of the ego.

But as we already know, the ego is just an illusion.

So let us take the ego out of the equation. What we have left is the truth and a world of enlightenment.

What does it mean to live in a world of enlightenment? It means that you are no longer in yourself mentally, living in an illusion.

DIAGRAM 34

You no longer need or want. You no longer search, because there is no need to. You are egoless, so there is no part of you that is separate from God.

You are in the total or complete form, one with the *I am*, spirit, God. This is living as one. This presence allows you to be one with all. You no longer are unattached.

If you fall back into the old patterns of the ego, you will sense the detachment from God and living life freely. Being oblivious to reality has again placed you in a world of opposites and dynamic drama.

So now that we understand what reality truly is, we clearly have a choice: peace or chaos.

Trust what you know, not what you were taught. If we say, "God is immeasurable," then God is all. If God is all, then aren't we a part of that? Physically, we are never detached from God—we never were.

DIAGRAM 34

Now, you must choose to awake to this reality or stay asleep. This is the choice of enlightenment or suffering.

DIAGRAM 35

# The Meaning of Life.

Diagram 35

## *The Meaning of Life*

Once upon a time, there was an immense playground. This playground contained an array of environments. There were jungles, forests, deserts, oceans, and mountains. It also contained countless animals and plants.

One day three children came upon this playground and stood in wonder of its greatness.

The first child ran as fast as she could and jumped, climbed, and played with all that she encountered. Every day she enjoyed the endless natural resources of food. Every day was a new adventure. She played and was at peace.

The second child ran out into the playground and played. But one day she began to think, *What is this plant? Does this fruit taste better than that one?*

She started to examine the plants and animals and eventually got lost within her endless list of questions. In her analyzing and

DIAGRAM 35

searching, she was never completely satisfied, never at peace.

The third child ran out into the playground
and played. But one day, after talking to the
second child, she found a particular yellow
fruit that tasted better than most of the other
fruits. So the third child fenced in an area of
yellow fruit all for herself.

She also found that the second child valued
cows, chickens, and pigs as a good food
source. So she quickly captured all the cows,
chickens, and pigs in the land.

Over many years, she gathered, managed,
and controlled all the food she could find.
She concentrated solely on ownership but
found it was never enough. She never had
enough. She was never at peace.

Which one sounds most like the history of
humankind?

Which one would you choose to be?

# *Where Do We Go from Here?*

Nowhere. Here is perfect.

If you find yourself slipping back into the same egocentric patterns, be still. That is...still your mind.

If you feel that you still need a map to find your way, you may find these additional comments helpful.

- Don't judge yourself or others. Let each other be. (Thoughts reflect values, values create needs, needs create frustration.)

- If you must react to someone else's action, first ask, "What is the intent of their action?"

- Be present in the moment. This is the only place to find true peace.

- Be of no mind. Engage in sincere action.

- Question your thoughts and actions. That is, think critically about why you do what you do.

- Write down your realizations and reflect upon them.

- Be thankful. Enjoy life. Be happy!

*Here is perfect.*